# The New Student

Written by **Melaina Faranda**
Illustrated by **QBS Learning**

# Fast phonics

Before reading this book, ask the student to practise saying the sounds (phonemes) and reading the new words used in the book. Try to make it as speedy and as fun as possible.

## Read the tricky high frequency words

The student can't sound out these words at the moment, but they need to know them because they are commonly used.

| use | used | your | here |

**Tip:** Encourage the student to sound out any sounds they know in these words, and you can provide them with the irregular or tricky part.

---

## Say the sounds

**u** unicorn
**u-e** cube

**ew** stew
**ue** rescue
**ay** play

**a** paper
**a-e** plane
**o** yo-yo

**Tip:** Remember to say the pure sounds. For example, 'ssss' and 'nnnn'. If you need a reminder, watch the *Snappy Sounds* videos.

## Snappy words

Point at a word randomly and have the student read the word. The student will need to sound out the word and blend the sounds to read the word. For example: 't–u–lll–i–p, tulip'.

| Duke | cute | unit |
| unicorn | student | tutor |
| Stu | cube | volume |
| human | tulip | music |
| tune | mute | computer |
| include | continue | Tuesday |
| rescue | | |

## Quick vocabulary check

The underlined words may not be familiar to the student. Check their understanding before you start to read the book.

"We have a new student," Miss Tulip said. "Meet Stu."

Duke didn't look up.

"Duke, can you be Stu's computer tutor?" Miss Tulip said. "He will need to use the computer for this unit."

Duke didn't seem keen. "But Miss Tulip, Stu is not human. Unicorns don't use computers!" he said.

Stu is a cute unicorn.

"We include all our students here, Duke. Continue to use the computers, students. Your projects are due on Tuesday," Miss Tulip said.

The students didn't argue with Miss Tulip.

Duke tried to tutor the new student, but it didn't help.

Stu's horn slipped on the computer. It turned the volume all the way up.

"Duke, I told you to help Stu to use the computer," Miss Tulip said. "Didn't you hear me?"

"Yes, Miss Tulip, but Stu is a unicorn! He cannot use a computer!"

Miss Tulip didn't like it when students argued.

Duke had to stay in during the break to make a cube on the computer.

During the break, Stu had fun.

The students brushed his mane.

Stu used his horn to skewer food.

The bell rang.

The students rushed back for music with Miss Tulip.

Stu sat next to Duke.

Duke had to tune everything. He tried to help Stu, but Stu's music was bad.

The volume made Miss Tulip's brain hurt.

Oh, rescue me. Can I press mute?

Duke led Stu to the drum kit room.

Stu used his horn as a drum stick. He was amazing!

Can you be my drum tutor?

Duke and Stu used the drum kit until the bell rang.

Miss Tulip came into the drum kit room. "How did it go for the new student?"

"Miss Tulip," Duke said, "can Stu sit with me again?"

Miss Tulip didn't argue.

# Comprehension questions

Well done!

### Let's talk about the story together

Ask the student:
- How did Duke feel about the unicorn at the beginning of the story? How did he feel at the end? Why do you think that?
- Which musical instrument was Stu very good at playing?
- What does the word 'cube' mean? Can you find a cube in the book?
- Have you ever been a new student before? What was it like?

### Snappy words

Ask the student to read these words as quickly as they can.

| | | |
|---|---|---|
| student | human | cube |
| volume | unit | tutor |
| tune | cute | music |

### Fluency

Can the student read the story again and improve on the last time?

Have fun!